Co[ntents]

3 The Gospel of Luke:
The Mission of Jesus and His Holy Spirit 39

4 The Gospel of John:
Union with Jesus and the Father 51

Foreword:
The Bible Was Written
to Be Read!

With much joy, people are rediscovering an old fact: the Bible was written to be read. God used human instruments to write his Word so that he could communicate with human beings. Scripture was intended to be understood. It was also intended to be interesting, enticing. It is. Its fascination for human beings continues because it is about life. If any book can be said to "tell it like it is," that book is the Holy Bible. It tells of the real experiences of real people who have real feelings. The central experience of these Biblical people is God in their ordinary lives. Scripture highlights the fact of God's participation in human life. Since this is a core issue for every person, Scripture captivates us. Increasingly, people come to the Bible for pleasure.

Scripture is also an invitation, with an RSVP. Reading it is uniquely interesting, because it invites every reader to say yes or no to the Father's creative work in his life and, ultimately, yes or no to Jesus Christ. Each reader of Scripture comes face-to-face with him and is urged to form a permanent, loving relationship with him.

So Scripture is an adventure God offers you. At the very least, the Book is thoroughly readable. At the most, it becomes part of your life which provides joy and challenge and comfort and guidance and understanding and inspiration. All this, between two covers. It awaits only your attention to begin to give you its gifts.

This booklet is a guide for your involvement in Scripture, especially the Gospels. Your response to the Biblical RSVP will remain entirely your own, but suggestions are given along the way. Suggestions include ideas for use in the family, questions for your stimulation, and possible time arrangements for classroom use. The booklet is not to be merely read. Its purpose requires that it be used, like the starter of a car. Experiment with the tips given. Let yourself experience your own responses.

Of course, the booklet is pointless alone. It depends on the Scripture to which it points. Use the booklet with the Bible right alongside. Read the references given. Make the booklet a companion to your Gospel reading, and the Gospels a companion to the booklet.

Finally — enjoy! Read with a light heart. Expect to have fun — fun in discovery, delight in learning, pleasure in prayer. Allow the Word of God into your own depths. Look for the human feeling, the familiar questions, the ordinary emotion, the action of God. As the Bible was written about people like you, so it was written for people like you. Through the Scripture, God asks to be a living part of your living.

The Four Gospels: Memories of the Early Church

The Gospels are unique in literature. No other kind of writing tries to accomplish its purpose in the same particular way. The purpose of the Gospels is to encourage you and me to believe in Jesus Christ, as John 20:31 tells us. Their singular method was the recording of the memories of the early Christian community, through the hearts, prayers, and minds of four individuals and their annotators. The motivation was God's mysterious process of inspiration.

How and Why the Gospels Were Written

The memories in the Gospels are not simply individual reminiscences but remembrances of the *Christian community.* Only John's Gospel was possibly written by an eyewitness. The Gospels are the recollections of a community of people for whom those recollections were life-changing. The community was recalling a Person and events which had molded them individually and together. For them nothing was the same after Jesus as it had been before him. Their memory of him was much more than affectionate recall. It was the core of their living.

Now pause a moment. How do you participate in your own strongest memories? Most of us experience several things when we remember. We know the facts, at least as they appeared to us at the time. We also re-experience the emotions that accompanied those factual events. We bring to mind again the significance of both facts and feelings. We recognize the effects the events had on our personality, our choices, our life. Our remembered perceptions of the event are also likely better. We grasp more clearly the central beauty and special gifts of the person or event. When we re-experience a memory, all these meanings become part of the original experience. Consequently, memories are never merely facts. Sometimes their significance attaches more to the meaning of the fact than to the fact itself. It is the content for living which we remember. So the question for Gospel readers is not "Did it really happen like that?" but rather, *"What import did the writer find in the event as he described it?"* The real question is often the harder one to answer, but it is more true to the Word of God — and much more rewarding to us.

Thus the Gospels are memories of the early Christian community, collected and written down in prayer and love by four different *writers and their annotators.* In those days, literature was not given copyrights nor considered inviolate at another hand. Just as a Gospel writer was inspired to his writing, so annotators (called, in Biblical scholarship, redactors or editors) came along to make additions and corrections in his work. It is the task of scholars to sort these out, but few of their conclusions affect the substance of what we in this booklet are seeking. For us now the significance of such scholarship is the reaffirmation of the communal nature of the Gospels, even from their earliest beginnings. Their single-name titles tell us that one person was the chief writer, but we know he used community material and others edited his book after him. Our society is so individualistic that we may at first have difficulty appreciating this community work. Yet we are learning that individual discernment is limited and that a committed community may well be a more reliable vessel of truth. So communal memory birthed the Gospels.

Finally, we bear in mind that the collecting, the writing and redaction (or editing) were guided by God through *inspiration.* No one seems to be able to explain exactly how inspiration operates. But through it God ensures that truth which really matters is present and recognizable in the Bible. Inspiration has also given the Scripture its vitality. It never gets old. It is always ahead of us and seems to speak to our precise need at any moment of openness. Jesus Christ is still reachable through the Gospel pages.

Evolution of the Four Gospels

As noted above, the first Christians did not turn immediately to pen and papyrus after Jesus ascended. Even though he had corrected their first expectations about an earthly kingdom, they now anticipated his early return. Probably none of them expected to die before he came back to them on earth. Their memories of his life, death, Resurrection were now the center of their prayer, their thought, all their activity. Their excitement knew no bounds. They hurried out to tell everyone as quickly as possible about Jesus. They preached and taught and healed. They attracted many people to the Lord. The Christian community was on its way.

But they did not write for years. Why? Because in that time, writing was not the most efficient means of communication. The disciples assumed they didn't have time to make written records before Jesus' return. The possible importance of recording for future generations did not at first occur to them because they didn't expect any future generations. But as years went by, and the eyewitnesses to Jesus' life on earth died or were martyred, the community began to gather their recollections. We are not able to reconstruct this process in much detail. But we do know that between A.D. 65 and 90 their collection and recording eventuated in our Gospels. Written initially by four individual Christians in quite different circumstances, the Gospels reflect various views and concerns. Each writer had his own group in mind, but each aimed primarily to inspire belief in Jesus.

If we were interested in Jesus from only one viewpoint, the four views we have would be a problem. But as we care about meaning and implication for our living, the multiple viewpoint is a big help. The first Gospel was written over 30 years after the time of Jesus. And from that first Gospel to the last nearly another 30 years elapsed. Circumstances and understandings change over such periods of time. We too change and grow. The Gospels have something to offer for every place along our road.

All the Gospels share primary material and basic convictions about the life, death, and Resurrection of Jesus. Yet they are diverse. Each one sees Jesus from a slightly different viewpoint. Our portrait of Jesus would be only partial were it not for these variant images. The point can be made by thinking of your own family. Who is the father? What is he like? Does the mother describe him in the same way as the oldest child? The youngest? How does he appear to his grandmother or his best friend? If you want a complete picture of the father, you ask for all these perspectives. The Gospels offer us a similarly complete portrait. Taken together, even the variations help provide our picture of Jesus Christ, the Son of God, who has something to say to us.

Since each Gospel was written by different people, we wonder if they have any relationship to each other. Only a little comparison shows that Matthew, Mark, and Luke are closely related in the literary sense. Matthew and Luke are both longer than Mark. They both contain most of the Marcan material. Matthew and Luke also have some material in common which Mark does not cover. Matthew gives us unique items, as does also Luke. Matthew and Luke are probably partially dependent on Mark. John, on the other hand, is apparently an independent production. Its outline is altogether distinct, and much if not most of John's material is exclusively his own. As we look at each Gospel separately in coming chapters, the particular themes and emphases of each one will be indicated.

The Goal of the Gospels

As you work through this booklet, you will quickly recognize that it is a very incomplete treatment of the Gospels. Just to imagine what "completeness" might involve, note the fact that Father Raymond Brown's commentary on the Gospel of John alone fills two big volumes. The purpose of this booklet is limited and specific: to *introduce* you to the reading and praying of

Scripture, to *lead you into* the Gospels. It is intended that through this booklet you will discover how to read the story of Jesus with joy and a sense of immediacy. You will also find here ways to use the Bible as a basis and content for your own prayer. It has been truly said that you cannot know the Scriptures until you have prayed them. All the study and all the background in all the libraries will not give you the insight that praying the Bible will give you. Through such inner knowledge you will come to know and love Jesus Christ intimately. That is the goal of the Gospels.

Think not for a moment that Jesus Christ is uninterested in your reading and praying the Gospels. If you are tantalized by them, it is because he has already invited you to himself. You are already responding to his invitation. You are to be commended for your sensitivity to him within you. Since he is vitally interested in your participation in Scripture, you may count on his aid. He will help you to understand its meanings, to perceive its purposes. He will be present to create within you the deeper love for himself that he wishes you to enjoy. God's continuing desire to communicate himself to people is the essence of all Scripture, both as it was written and also now as it is read. He wants you to understand.

Suggestions for Reading and Praying

Family suggestions. Reading and praying the Scripture together is an experience no family should miss. It is an ideal way to deepen our oneness with the Lord and with one another. Family reading and praying of the Bible deepens true human and spiritual communication among family members. It helps us to live as loving and hope-filled Christians.

Here are some general suggestions that can enrich your family participation in Scripture:

1. Read the Bible and pray together *regularly.* How often and how long will vary with each family. Together, choose your times. Then make it a point to be faithful to these agreed-upon meetings.

Before the main meal of the day is a good time for a brief reading of a favorite Gospel passage. After the reading, your meal prayer together can be based on what the Lord has communicated to you in the Scripture.

A longer session at least once a week is also suggested. Saturday and Sunday evenings are good times for these get-togethers. Remember that these are special moments in the life of your family — times when you deliberately choose to be together to love one another by sharing the Word of God.

2. Let the children do as much as possible; active involvement is the key to maintaining their interest. Always make these times a joyful experience for the children; in later life, their memories of these get-togethers will have a profound influence on their relationships with you and with God.

3. When you meet to read and pray, have two dictionaries on hand: a regular one and a Bible dictionary. One of the most useful and inexpensive of the latter is *The New World Dictionary-Concordance to the New American Bible,* a paperback book by World Publishing (2080 W. 117th Street, Cleveland, OH 44111). When you come to a word you don't know, stop and look it up.

4. Experiment with memorizing favorite passages. This discipline is a wonderful gift for your children's adulthood — and for your own.

5. There are many excellent materials available that can enrich your appreciation of the Gospels. The following are recommended:

For younger children, Regina Press publishes a series of small, colorful books with simple words. Some of the titles are: *New Testament for Children, The Life of Jesus for Children, The Friends of Jesus for Children, The Miracles of Jesus for Children, Bible Prayers for Children.* (These books are available from Liguori Publications.)

For older children, the American Bible Society (1865 Broadway, New York, NY 10023) publishes *The Children's*

Bible, an easy-to-read collection of Bible passages with color illustrations.

An excellent series of pictures for children of any age is "Bible Teaching Pictures" by Richard Hook, available from David C. Cook Publishing Company (850 N. Grove Ave., Elgin, IL 60120).

Learning about Jesus, a paperback booklet available from Liguori Publications, features 12 Gospel playlets that young family members can perform at home.

6. Prayer should be a part of every family meeting with the Bible. After reading and discussion, lay everything aside and give each family member a chance simply to talk to Jesus. Take turns talking to him in your own words. If the Spirit moves the group to pray in silence, that too is very good. (A note to parents: During these times of spontaneous prayer, resist any temptation to deliver little sermons for the children's benefit!)

At times you may want to end your session with a brief Bible prayer service. A good book for this purpose is *Discovering the Bible,* available from Liguori Publications. In addition to learning material, the book contains 17 brief prayer services, each based on a Scripture reading and group responses from the Psalms.

7. As you go through this booklet, let the family set its own pace. At all times, don't forget: Laugh together, be amazed together, rejoice together over your discoveries in God's Word.

Class group suggestions. If you are a group using this booklet in class, here are two optional ways of structuring your sessions.

For a 10-session series: The first session would be general introduction, using pages 7-14, the introductory part of this booklet. The last session would be review and filling in any obvious gaps. Two sessions would be devoted to each Gospel. The breakdown goes like this:

Session 1: An introductory session, using this Introduction (pages 7-14 of this booklet).

Sessions 2 and 3: The Gospel of Mark (chapter 1 of this booklet).

Sessions 4 and 5: The Gospel of Matthew (chapter 2 of this booklet).

Sessions 6 and 7: The Gospel of Luke (chapter 3 of this booklet).

Sessions 8 and 9: The Gospel of John (chapter 4 of this booklet).

Session 10: A review of each Gospel, highlighting whatever your group has found to be most meaningful, and filling in any gaps you want to focus on.

For a 20-session series: The first and last sessions would be the same as in the 10-session series. Each Gospel could receive four or five sessions, depending on the group's interest.

Now let's begin our exploration of early Christian memories with the Gospel of Mark.

Remember to enjoy . . .

1
The Gospel of Mark: The Person, Jesus

The Gospel of Mark is the shortest Gospel. Yet many people like it best because of its uncomplicated, straightforward presentation of the actions of Jesus. Of Mark's 16 chapters, 13½ are devoted to the Lord's public ministry. A few verses speak of John the Baptizer and Jesus' preparation for ministry; and 2½ chapters recount the Passion and Resurrection. If you want to treat yourself to an encounter with Jesus the doer, read the whole Gospel of Mark at one sitting.

Date and Author

It is generally agreed that Mark was the first Gospel written. Early tradition — attested at the beginning of the second century — tells us that the writer was one John Mark who had not known Jesus personally, but who was very close to Peter. (If this is the same John Mark mentioned in Acts and Paul's letters, then he was also Barnabas' cousin and well known to Paul.) If Mark followed Peter, listened to him reminisce about Jesus, heard him preach, then we may have a recounting of Peter's recollections as Mark remembered them. Mark likely wrote after Peter's death in 64 A.D. As well as Peter's memory, Mark probably used other sources. Certainly he had heard preaching and reminiscences from other Christians.

No one is sure where Mark himself came from. His double name, one Jewish and one Greek, may indicate he was a Jew raised outside of Palestine. His Gospel contains no hint that Palestine was his original home. The people for whom he writes are Gentiles rather than Jews, probably Christians in Rome. His story of Jesus shows almost no interest in connections with the Old Testament. For Gentiles such connections would hardly be

15

helpful. But he does explain some things which Romans and other Gentiles might not know, such as geography in Palestine (11:1), Aramaic words (5:41 or 10:46), and unusual Jewish customs (7:3-4). You will find other similar explanations as you read; in fact, they will be helpful to you, as you too are a Gentile not born in first-century Palestine.

Circumstances and Audience

To understand Mark's purposes, let's recall what was happening to the Christian community during the 60s A.D. First of all, Jesus had not returned when they expected. They had been anticipating, praying, yearning for a whole generation since Jesus' Ascension. Those who had known him in his public ministry, who had seen the Risen Jesus with their own eyes, were dying. When would Jesus come back? Would he come at all? How can we understand the long delay? These were hard questions for new Christians. One of Mark's purposes is to bolster their confidence in Jesus as a person, to strengthen their faith in who he was, regardless of the time of his return. The chapter which discusses his return is chapter 13. You may want to read it over. You will find signs and predictions, but nothing concretely identifiable. The attitude to be taken by Jesus' followers, however, is clear: be watchful and don't be gullible about false claims. This is an attitude we still try to foster today, when many are predicting the time of Jesus' return.

Another big issue for Gentile Christians was their standing in the eyes of the Roman government. In the 60s persecutions were arising in various places and were especially serious in Rome during Nero's reign. Among the many martyred at this time were Peter and probably Paul. How were Christians to withstand terrorized living? Could they remain loyal to Jesus under threat of torture? How could they live with suffering when it came? How could they face death itself? Nero's persecution of Christians in the 60s may have been one of his several aberrations, but Christians were a legally unrecognized group.

Although they were not actively hunted, they definitely were subject to criminal penalties. Seeing these circumstances, Mark accentuated those aspects of Jesus' character and work which would strengthen his followers.

So Mark records a collection of memories, perhaps chiefly Peter's. He tells his stories creatively, grounded in accurate recounting of earlier tradition, but arranged to speak to the hearts of people who believe in Jesus and have to wait longer for his return, possibly facing persecution. What, then, did Mark say about Jesus that would help these people? What does he say that can help us?

Jesus, Son of Man

Mark portrays Jesus from several angles: as the Son of Man, as a miracle worker, as the Messiah and Son of God. Let's look at each of these in turn.

In Mark, Jesus calls himself "Son of Man" in several passages: Mark 2:10,28; 8:31-38; 9:9,12,31; 10:33-45. In these statements Jesus seems to use the title in the same way it is used in the Old Testament generally: to mean a son of a man, or simply a human being. Later in Mark, Jesus may be suggesting a more far-reaching significance in the title. Read Mark 13:26; 14:21; 14:42,62. Here Jesus may be referring back to the Book of Daniel where the prophet sees a vision of great things to come. Compare Daniel 7:13 with the latter series of verses. The similarity might hint at what Jesus himself anticipated. It certainly suggests what Mark understood to be Jesus' rightful position.

While intimating an exalted status as Son of Man, Mark nevertheless emphasizes Jesus' humanity. Especially in this Gospel Jesus is an appealing person, one we can feel close to because he has feelings and does human things. In the very first chapter, beginning with verse 40, Mark shows that Jesus does not heal nonchalantly. He feels for the hurting one, he experiences an inner response. In compassion he reaches out to give what he has. Or again in 3:1-5, Jesus feels anger and deep grief at the narrowness of the religious leadership. He is not a cold, distant man who is righteous. He is a warm, sensitive human who responds with fervor to the people around him.

In 4:35-39, Jesus is sailing with his fishermen friends and they nearly sink in a squall. But Jesus is asleep on a cushion. Isn't there a certain endearment about a sleeping person, a bit of vulnerability? What does it tell us about Jesus? He must have been very tired, needing rest so badly that even the storm didn't waken him. He must have been at peace with himself or he'd have slept more lightly. Nor is he here the great ascetic — he sleeps on a pillow like the rest of us prefer. This Jesus we can touch with our hearts.

Discover for yourself the other phrases in Mark which speak warmly of Jesus' humanity. Maybe underscore them with a colored highliner. Or jot down in the margin your own response to his feelings. Would you share them? Would you want to comfort him? Would you cheer for him? When you have found all the references, you might share your feelings with your family or your class. Then, individually or together, take your responses into prayer. He is still alive, still warm and open to your feelings for him. Express them to him now, simply and honestly. "I couldn't do it for you then, Lord, but now I will cheer you up!"

Throughout Mark the caring Son of Man is also strong and authoritative. Note the dispatch with which he works. Jesus intends a result; it happens. For example, see Mark 1:29-31. But more explicitly, Jesus' authority is brought out by his own statements and deeds, as well as by the reactions of the people. Read Mark 2:6-12 and 2:23-28.

Look also at Mark 1:22. Have you ever known persons who spoke with authority? They are rare. I have known one. He does not merely propound what he's been taught nor repeat what he has read. He speaks with authority because all he says has been hammered out of his own painful experience, deeply pondered. Jesus could speak with authority of the Father and the Kingdom because he knew the Father firsthand and he lived in the Kingdom. When people questioned his right to authority over the Sabbath (Mark 2:27-28) or the Law (7:1-20) or the Temple (11:15-18), Jesus simply acted. His power was only a demonstration of his prior authority.

The issue of authority climaxes in Mark 11:27-33. The Temple officials challenge Jesus. Perhaps they had never known a person with genuine authority — although, of course, their direct challenge was prompted by the chaos he had caused previously in the Temple (see Mark 11:15-16). So they demanded his credentials. He doubtless knew it was a trap, but he recognized too that real authority is its own credential, which only time will vindicate. It must have required total confidence and unparalleled inner poise to refuse to answer the priests.

Today some authority is given by status in life or by the weapon one carries or by the garb one wears. Some authority is delegated by people who agree to be subject to it. Some authority is usurped by might. But Jesus' authority was altogether different. It was personal authority. The people who first recognized his authority did not know who he was. They could not have thought "He is God, therefore he has authority." Rather, their perception of his authority led them in time to believe that he was man fully developed, and more than man as well.

Jesus, the Miracle Worker

Another spectacular aspect of Jesus in Mark is the miracles he worked. The Gospel almost seems to rush from one astounding event to another. If we weren't so jaded by familiarity and analysis, our mouths would open in wonder. Perhaps so would our minds.

You may want to scan the Gospel again to determine how much of it reports Jesus' miracles. Half? Two thirds? In Mark, the teachings of Jesus take a secondary place. What is Mark trying to say by stressing Jesus' power? That he had authority, certainly. That he was able to *do* what was needed in people's lives. But more, Mark is saying: Look at this *Person*. He is neither a vague idea nor a mythological figure. He is a person who behaves in certain ways and has a describable personality. Mark is urging us, *Look at Jesus!* His miracles are acts of compassion and demonstrations of power, yes, but they are also intended to make us do a double take with our whole selves. Look again at this Jesus. Probe to find out who he is. Then — come share our belief and our commitment to him. That is what Mark wants.

Jesus, the Messiah

Of course, total commitment can finally be made only to God, hardly to a mere human being. Mark does not ignore the relationship of Jesus to God the Father. He never calls Jesus "God" outright. Mark calls him "Messiah" only three times. The coming of a messiah (meaning anointed one) was a strictly Jewish concept. To the Jews it included a whole complex of expectations: history was to be ended by the direct action of God who would anoint his Holy One to rule this world thereafter; Israel would be the center of the new age, and the Anointed One would be all their own; other nations would flow to Jerusalem motivated by desire for Israel's God; Israel would wield controlling political power (a natural hope after centuries of political dependency). None of these dreams meant anything to Gentiles. So a Gospel written for Gentiles does not emphasize them. Of the three situations in which Mark calls Jesus the Messiah, two are completely Jewish: when Peter tells Jesus who he thinks Jesus is (Mark 8:27-29) and during Jesus' trial before the Jewish high priest (Mark 14:61-62).

The Jewish concept of Messiah does play a part in Mark, but only as background for understanding. We find it in what scholars call the "messianic secret." In Mark, Jesus repeatedly warns recipients of his miracles, the evil spirits themselves, and even his own followers that they must not tell anyone who he is. See Mark 7:36, for example.

Why didn't Jesus want people to know who he was? The answer may lie in the Jewish expectation of a political power-ruler. Jesus rejected this view of himself and had no intention of letting people push him into it. His was a different method. When Peter protests his Master's prediction about future suffering, Jesus rebukes him sharply (Mark 8:31-33). Consistently then, Jesus urges people not to spread the word about him too soon and arouse revolutionary hopes in which he would not participate. Jesus is in reality protecting his people (as well as himself and his true purpose) from false expectations.

Jesus, the Son of God

Jesus' relationship to the Father is expressed by Mark as Son of God or Holy One of God (see Mark 1:1; 1:11; 1:24; 3:11; 5:7; 9:7; 14:61-62; 15:39). This title had meaning in Hellenistic (Greek or Greek-influenced) religious notions. Many cults of the Greco-Roman world envisioned a kind of emanation from the divine which would take on human form temporarily and be called a son of god. But Jesus is not an emanation, and his human nature was not temporary. Mark makes this quite clear through Jesus' authority over virtually everything and through his human emotional life. Moreover, while calling him Son of God, Mark emphasizes the suffering of Jesus — certainly not the Hellenistic notion of divine emanation. Neither was it the common notion of the Jewish Messiah. Mark insists that Jesus' real nature as Son of God may be perceived through his actual suffering and his Resurrection. In this suffering Son of God, Christians found and still find strength to face injustice and persecution.

During his public work, Jesus predicts and tries to explain his impending suffering to his closest followers. They either reject it, like Peter, or do not understand. See Mark 9:31-32. Jesus has painful moments during his ministry. See Mark 6:5-6; 8:14-21. But of course, the deepest suffering he undergoes just before his death. Beginning in Mark 14:32, Jesus' agony is the whole of Mark's concern. Reread this description of the Passion. Be careful not to read your previous knowledge into this story. Read it just for what it is here in Mark. Notice the constant movement, the poignancy of Jesus' few comments, the crass injustice of his trials, and his quiet composure under harassment, the insults lasting to the final moment. And at his death, note the ultimate crushing human anguish — the feeling that even the Father had abandoned him. Mark tells it starkly with no frills and few explanations, letting our own hearts ask what it all meant to Jesus.

Mark's treatment of the Resurrection is brief, focusing largely on the responses and long-term tasks of Jesus' followers. Did he think the bare statement of Jesus' rising from the dead was enough? Or has something been lost? We don't know. But we can be grateful for the magnificent picture of Jesus, Son of Man and Son of God, which Mark has drawn for us with such forceful and revealing strokes.

Praying with Mark

Since Mark features the person of Jesus, our prayer with Mark best follows that theme. Mark obviously enjoyed writing about Jesus. His love for Jesus shows in his attention to detail. If we look lovingly at those same details, we will find ourselves with Jesus. That is prayer enough.

So, as a beginning, let's simply enjoy Jesus. Use your favorite incident from the Gospel. One of my own favorites is Jesus with the children (see Mark 9:36 and 10:13-16). What makes a more delightful scene than a strong man, gentle with a child? Jesus holds the children in his arms, touches them, blesses them. Can't you just see him brushing a wisp of hair from a youngster's eyes? Wouldn't his face be alight with joy in their beauty? Wouldn't he be laughing at their antics, smiling tenderly at their shyness? Isn't he a beautiful person, the kind you would thoroughly enjoy in your own home? If you want to invite him in, you are praying already.

A wonderful thing about Jesus is that all he was on earth is available to us now in the Risen Jesus. He took it all with him. We have even more than those earthly companions had, because we understand better who he is. But many persons have concentrated so hard on Jesus' divinity that they do not see his splendid humanity. Reading and praying with Mark can balance that. It is the human Jesus who inspires devotion and tenderness within us.

So ponder Mark's stories of Jesus' public ministry and take pleasure in Jesus. Choose your favorite incident. Read it over and over, slowly and feelingly. Visualize it in your mind as completely as you can. Ask yourself: What does he look like? What colors does he wear? What gestures or expressions are his? What is his voice like? Is the scene in a village? Trees around? Barren hillside with rocks or maybe sheep? Dusty road? Bright hot sun? Cool breeze?

Now put yourself in the scene. Go near enough to see Jesus well. Watch him the way you would watch any fascinating person. Do him a favor — pay him a compliment, bring him a little water. How does he respond to you? Do you enjoy his comment to you? Do you like him? Is his warmth alive in your spirit? And if you want to hug him for sheer delight in his charm, please do. Then relax a while, comfortable as you are with anyone you love and who loves you. Be glad to share a moment of life with him. He will be glad to share it with you. If you think it is all your imagination, you are mistaken. Somewhere along the way, he has come to your heart, where the two of you can be at one, smiling into each other's eyes.

Creating a dialogue with Jesus is another fine method of prayer with Mark. Perhaps you will choose the story in Mark 10:17-31 where Jesus is already conversing. Put yourself in that group, and ask the questions that come to your mind. Participate. Speak to Jesus directly. See him turn to you and answer. Listen to him. Reply to him. Listen again. Let your dialogue go where it will, remembering the Jesus of Mark, the feeling, responsive, human Jesus. You may find this difficult to do all in your head; you may prefer a written dialogue. Write in a relaxed way, using the same approach as for the purely mental dialogue. You may find yourself asking him about your present problems. That's fine. Expect to appreciate what he tells you. He may surprise you!

These simple methods of prayer can become very deep experiences. They can reveal to you both Jesus and yourself. Best of all, Jesus will become increasingly a real person to you, as he was to Mark and all the early Christians.

Visualization and dialogue can be shared with your family or class. Since each person's imagination, capacity for visualization, and creative dialogue are individual, you may practice first alone. Share afterwards. You parents may be startled at what Jesus says to your children; your children may be thrilled at what you say to him. One thing is certain: if you share your experiences with Jesus among yourselves at home, you will grow together in your love for him and for each other.

The same will happen in a class. Shared experience of Jesus will change you from a group of people gazing at the same study material to a community of love and openness. Jesus has a way of doing that, even when he works through our own imaginations. Let him, won't you?

Questions to Answer

Note: As you answer the questions given here and in the following chapters, be specific. *Jot down the references from which your answers come.* Do not answer merely from "feelings" you already have about Jesus; make your answers come from the Gospel. Answering in this way will clarify both your own thought and your understanding of the Gospel itself.

If you are in a group, use the questions for discussion. Take time to look up the references each person has found. *Don't hesitate to write in your Bible.* No one will remember everything in the readings, so note your responses in the margins.

1. What kind of a man was Jesus? List 15 words that describe him. (If you are a class or a family, refine the list until your description satisfies everybody.)

2. How did the crowds react to Jesus' words and actions?

3. How did the Jewish leaders react to him? Did they have any reasons for their reactions?

4. Can you find anything in Mark about Jesus' daily life? What did he do with his time? Look for details.

5. As you read Mark, follow the development of the conflict that ends with Jesus' death. This theme reads almost like a detective story. Can you summarize it in your own words?

6. How does Jesus heal? Does he lay down any conditions? What motivates him? Does he ever refuse anyone?

Suggestions for Family Use

Use any of the suggestions you find in this chapter, including the ones under the next heading, "Session Suggestions."

Children are great "imaginers." When you are focusing on a particular story, encourage the children to set the scene in detail. After one child describes the setting, have another add to it. Have them take turns giving details of what takes place. When it comes time for family prayer, use ideas that the children came up with.

Look up words like *authority, Messiah, miracle* in your regular dictionary and Bible dictionary. Do the words you looked up have the same meaning today that they had in Jesus' day?

Here are some family discussion questions. Support your answers with stories from Mark.

● What was Jesus like when he walked the earth? If you had been with Jesus then, would you have liked him? Why?

● Is Jesus the same today as he was then? If so, how? Is he different in any way?

Create a family dialogue. First, make up a situation. For example: What would happen if Jesus came to our home for dinner? Or: What would it be like if Jesus came with us on a family outing?

Now reflect out loud together about what Jesus would do and say, what you would do and say. Keep it detailed. Enjoy his being with you.

Session Suggestions

If you are using this booklet for a 10-session series, here are suggestions for the two sessions on Mark.

Session 1: First, read the whole Gospel of Mark once. Then read this booklet chapter, looking up the suggested references in Mark. These two readings will give you a feeling for Mark and a general picture of Jesus. (Set a time limit so that the reading doesn't take too long.) Then privately pray as suggested in the section "Praying with Mark." Finally, as the core of the session, share your reactions and prayer experiences.

Session 2: Focus on answering the six questions above in the section "Questions to Answer." Then pray as suggested in "Praying with Mark" and share.

If you are using this booklet for a 20-session series, here are suggestions for the four sessions on Mark.

Session 1: Read the whole Gospel of Mark once for general feeling and a general portrait of Jesus. Share responses and answer Question 1 in the section "Questions to Answer."

Session 2: Read this booklet chapter, marking and reading all the references given. Review and discuss these main ideas. Answer whatever questions the group raises.

Session 3: Read the Gospel of Mark through again. Pray as suggested in "Praying with Mark." Share reactions and prayer experiences.

Session 4: Read Mark again and answer Questions 2 through 6. You may want to assign several people to each question and have them report to the group. Discussion will flow naturally.

Always proceed lightheartedly, anticipating the adventure and the joy that Mark himself experienced in his love for Jesus. Keep it happy!

2
The Gospel of Matthew: The Teachings of Jesus

Like Mark, the Gospel of Matthew is Jesus-centered. But Matthew's purposes are angled differently and reflect both his own theology and the age and community to which he belonged.

The writer of Matthew must have been an interesting man himself. We know nothing definite about him, but scholars surmise from his carefully composed Gospel that he was a rabbi converted to Christianity. The rabbinical pattern of thought and argument is visible in Matthew's Jesus.

Date, Author, Circumstances, Audience

The date of Matthew's writing has been much debated. Matthew used Mark, as well as other materials and traditions, so the date would be after the 60s A.D. Also, Matthew mentions conditions in the Christian community and the world which appeared only after 70 A.D. On the basis of such facts, today's scholars generally agree that Matthew was written in the early 80s.

To enhance our understanding of Matthew's purpose, let's review the world of the 80s. Jesus has been gone for 50 years. Christians are Gentiles as well as Jews. The eyewitnesses to Jesus' earthly life are gone (except possibly John, son of Zebedee). Jesus' return is still longingly awaited. Christians have already suffered persecution at the hands of Roman emperors.

Meanwhile, relations between Romans and Jews had steadily worsened. Jewish determination to be free of the Roman yoke blossomed into a full-scale armed revolt in the late 60s. Rome finally lost patience and crushed the Jewish nation. In 70 A.D. the Temple was burned to the ground and Jerusalem became a broken city. Faced with such disaster, Jewish leaders of the

Pharisee party gathered in Jamnia in western Palestine to recoup their spiritual forces and define themselves, so that Judaism could survive. Now the growing strength of the Christian community seemed a serious threat to Judaism. So the Jews in council at Jamnia expelled Jewish Christians from the synagogue — the outcome of the long conflict between those Jews who accepted Jesus and those who did not.

Matthew, being a Jew converted to Christianity, writes especially for these Jewish Christians. He wants to establish the authority of Jesus as the Messiah of God and the Christian community as the true Israel and bearer of Jesus' authority. He parallels Jesus and the New Covenant with Moses and the Old Covenant. Just as Moses had given God's instruction to those specially covenanted to him, so Jesus gives God's instruction to those now newly convenanted to him. Jesus completes and transcends all that God had done before. See Matthew 5:17-20; 11:28; 12:21.

Matthew hopes to give the Jewish Christians a firm ground for belief, while also convincing other Jews that Jesus' way is the true way. So Matthew strongly emphasizes Jesus' teachings — teachings about God, about the Law, about how people could live. He arranges the teachings in discourses preceded by stories. Each narrative/discourse section centers around at least one primary issue.

Jesus' New Way of Living: The Sermon on the Mount

The first set of narratives (chapters 1-4) establishes Jesus' importance and authority: his descent from David (1:1-18) and from God (1:18ff); his parallel to Moses (2:13-23); John's witness to him as "the one who is to come" (chapter 3); the foundations of Jesus' own ministry (4:1-17); the beginnings of his "organization" (4:18-22); and a summary of his early work (4:23-25). On this groundwork Matthew presents the first discourse, the masterful Sermon on the Mount.

It isn't likely that the Sermon was ever delivered exactly as we have it. Jesus was too good a teacher to compress all his essential teachings into one short sermon. To us it is relatively familiar, but if we were hearing it spoken for the first time, our comprehension would cease somewhere about the fourth verse! So Matthew summarizes and condenses Jesus' foundational teachings, arranging them to be read rather than preached. Thanks to him, we can mull over Jesus' instructions at our own pace.

Mulling over is the least they will require. You can only approach chapters 5 through 7 of Matthew as a perpetual learner. If that's hard on your self-esteem, note that the attitude of the dependent learner is happily commended in the first "beatitude" (5:3).

Jesus' teachings are directions for living in his Kingdom. For Jesus, the predominant quality of Kingdom life is joyfulness; that's the meaning of "blessed." Pause to consider that.

Jesus lists the circumstances in which we find joy in the Kingdom (5:3-11). The list is a rough parallel in form to the Old Covenant (the Ten Commandments). Jesus does not intend to destroy the Old Law but to complete it. He utterly respects the Old Covenant with which he and his hearers grew up. But there is more, and he is here to give it to them.

Jesus' Attitudes and Ours

Jesus reveals the "more" he came to give by insisting that the visible act does not matter most, though it too is important. Rather, the inner state is supremely important. This concept may be as difficult for us as for Jesus' early listeners. How often have we said something like, "I was so mad I was boiling, but of course I didn't do anything." Old Law mentality, isn't it? Jesus tells us to go deeper — it's the inward that is real.

Is Jesus striking us with impossible demands? No. He's simply saying, "If you want to live joyously in my Kingdom, this is how you do it." He assures us elsewhere that he will supply the capacity, but we have to want it. So pray first to desire his Kingdom in your life now, then to be able to learn the Kingdom's "traffic rules."

The "traffic" in the Kingdom, Jesus says, flows best when we observe:

(1) reconciliation instead of anger (5:21-26);
(2) ruthlessness regarding our own sin (5:27-30);
(3) commitment to marriage (5:31-32);
(4) simplicity and directness (5:33-37);
(5) generosity regardless of circumstances (5:38-42);
(6) love for all equally, no matter what they've done (5:43-47);
(7) secrecy in good deeds (6:1-8).

Perhaps Matthew senses that such a concentrated challenge could be a bit overwhelming. So he recalls Jesus' teaching about singleness of intention, of having one goal and one master. Jesus urges us to order our lives by what is essential, rather than by the earth clutter around us. Do one thing, he insists: live in the Kingdom of joy (6:19-24).

But how? The world is still very much with us. Jesus tells us to do it by trusting the Father (6:25-34). Such trust is no abstraction, according to him. It pertains to very practical matters, including what you eat and wear. The Father will take care of those things, if you intend to live in the Kingdom and trust him so he can act for you. Can you imagine a freer way of life?

Then Jesus informs us that in the Kingdom, in the spiritual realm where he dwells, you get exactly what you give (7:1-5, 11). If you need power for giving better or for acquiring the attitudes in the Sermon, you need only ask (7:7-11). Last of all, Jesus cautions us. It isn't easy, and we must be completely sincere toward the Father — which is the only sensible way to go (7:13-27).

Jesus' Behavior and Ours

Naturally, if our attitudes are transformed into those of the Kingdom, our behavior will be transformed too. Likewise, we cannot force a change in our behavior without letting him alter our attitudes. Read again the following references, and note the action that results from the new attitude: 5:23-26; 5:34,37; 5:39-42; 5:44-46; 6:14-15; 7:1; 7:12.

Chapters 8 through 10 contain the next narrative/discourse. In chapters 8 and 9, Matthew tells story after story of Jesus' amazing ability to heal, to calm, to disregard social prejudices, to restore life. He demonstrates his authoritative power. Then in chapter 10, he passes on his power to his followers and tells them how to use it.

These instructions to his first missionaries were probably for a short-term mission, rather than a 2,000-year evangelization program. Yet we find principles which would strengthen our own witness to him. One is an attitude we've already been told is necessary to Kingdom life: trust. Witnesses are to trust that their material needs will be provided (10:10), that in trial the right words will be given them (10:19-20), and that they will be protected by the Father (10:29-30). Also they may be assured of troubles; placidity is not for the witness.

What freedom the Kingdom offers! Freedom to share Jesus, freedom to act fearlessly, freedom to live securely. Take a few moments to recall a time when you have felt freed. Let that feeling expand, filling your inner self. Turn to Jesus in trust, as asked of a witness. Explore with him what freedom could mean in your living. Is it alluring?

The Meaning of the Kingdom

In the next section, chapters 11 through 13, Jesus describes the Kingdom of God. The key to these chapters seems to be the query from John the Baptizer in 11:2-3. Jesus doesn't answer directly (good rabbinical style!), but points to his results. Then he shows further that his authority and his action are really one (chapter 12) and distinguishes between the evil kingdom and his own Kingdom (12:22-45).

In chapter 13 he explains in parables the nature of the

Kingdom. This method is not always understood, because we can find several meanings in a parable. Jesus' stories were probably intended to express a single idea, though subordinate ideas may sometimes be helpful. Let's look at one point from each parable:

Matthew 13:4-23: The Kingdom is offered to everyone, but only in a few does it root, grow, and bring harvest.

Matthew 13:24-30,36-43: Even in the Kingdom, as long as earth remains, there will be good people and bad people. It is only for God to separate them.

Matthew 13:31-35: The Kingdom has invisible, tiny beginnings, but will eventually affect all human living.

Matthew 13:44-46: Life in the Kingdom is worth any price. Even if one gives up everything else to gain the Kingdom, he is only being intelligent.

Jesus' final comment (13:52) is intriguing. Might it reflect the writer's picture of himself, since he was able to draw both from Jesus and from the Old Covenant?

Chapters 14 through 18 present a challenging discussion of the Kingdom as it is lived out in the Christian community. In the stories Jesus shows his compassion as well as its effectiveness (14:13-21; 15:21-39). He needs to be alone to pray (14:13, 22-23). His is power and authority (15:1-20). The episode of Peter on the water illustrates the dependence on Jesus which is faith (14:22-33). Chapter 16:13-28 urges Christians to a singleness of devotion to Jesus the Messiah, whose way is not the obvious. Then the series climaxes with the Transfiguration (17:1-8) and the disciples' lamentable inability to heal a boy in trouble (17:14-20). They are not yet dependent enough on the Father or on Jesus himself — and he shakes his head at them.

Now comes the main question: Who is greatest in the Kingdom? We have heard the answer until our sensitivities are jaded. Try to read chapter 18 as if it were entirely new to you. Here are instructions for life in Christian community; think what your own life will be like if you take them absolutely seriously. Constantly keep in mind 16:24-26.

The greatest in the Kingdom is the one most dependent on the Father (18:1-7,10). To become dependent, you must not yield to self-sufficiency (18:8-9). You must be free of all contempt, no matter how small others seem (18:10-14), because every human being is infinitely precious to the Father. There must be no divisions, no lack of reconciliation between Christians. Matthew gives procedures for correcting such situations (18:15-17). Note especially that a persistently fractious person is to be treated like a tax collector. How did Jesus treat tax collectors? He spent his time with them and he loved them into life.

Peter understands Jesus' instructions about forgiveness — almost! The old rabbinic rule said a person was obligated to forgive his wrongdoer four times. Peter sees that generosity is called for and suggests seven (18:22). But Jesus outstrips even that, saying there can be no limitation to forgiveness, neither because of the number of offenses nor because of their seriousness. To those who find forgiveness difficult, the story of the merciless servant (18:23-35) asserts unforgettably that no one is asked to forgive more than God has forgiven him. What about the torturers? Is the Father really so vindictive? Hardly. But the torturers are built into us. Anger releases toxins in our bodies and cherished anger keeps them flowing. Sooner or later we will be sick, though we may not connect our illness with an unforgiving spirit.

In chapters 19 through 22, Matthew packs every story with teachings as if hurrying to complete them. Chapters 23 through 25 are Jesus' discourse which includes his discussion of life in the Kingdom, its principles and outcome. Jesus is blunt about some things like divorce (19:3-12), followed significantly by reaffirmation of approval for the dependent one (19:13-15). The handicap of wealth in the Kingdom shocks his followers (19:16-30). In chapter 21, Jesus again asserts his authority over Jewish institutions and leadership, so they seek to trap him until (in 22:46) he proves altogether too clever at their own game. After that they leave him and plot behind his back.

Then in chapter 23 Jesus contrasts the attitudes and behavior of the Pharisees with the instructions he's been giving about the Kingdom. In chapter 24, his followers are warned to be watchful and patient in coming troubles. Chapter 25 culminates in two parables which insist that people must bear the fruit of love, whether or not they recognize Jesus. Chapter 25:31-46 is really a restatement of 12:50. Jesus encourages his followers to adopt an attitude of alert trustfulness and to do the Father's will. Then they will be with him in the fulfillment of the Kingdom.

The final three chapters (26 through 28) tell of Jesus' suffering, crucifixion and death, and his Resurrection. These chapters can be freshly read in the light of all Jesus has taught. Compare his teaching with his attitudes and behavior during his Passion. Does he practice what he has preached? Explore for yourself by finding in earlier chapters the teachings which match his actions in chapters 26 through 28.

As for joy in the Kingdom, isn't the Resurrection the full flowering of that joy? If we have experienced Jesus even a little, what more do we desire than Matthew 28:20?

Praying with Matthew

Prayer with Matthew is active prayer. Its foundation is personal contact with Jesus. The key to prayer with Matthew is given in 5:6 and 7:7-8: hunger for goodness and persistent petition.

Let's begin with petition and with inner attitudes. Let's trust as in 6:25-34 and let go our material concerns, even if only for an hour. Then we will be freer to ask for, to seek deeply, to petition Jesus persistently for growth.

We begin with inner attitudes. We only damage ourselves when we try to produce good behavior while clinging to attitudes inconsistent with Jesus. For example, if we do good deeds for pride's sake, we are creating conflict within ourselves. We are lying to the Lord. We thus construct a beam for our eye that prevents us from perceiving truth.

One way of asking Jesus to help with attitudes is to ponder the discourses in Matthew (chapters 5 through 7; chapters 10, 13, and 18; chapters 23 through 25). Do not examine your conscience in your usual way. Just relax and be alert to your inner self, where he will be speaking to you. Let him indicate where to begin. Be dependent, helpless like a youngster who can't yet dress himself. Say, "Lord, I cannot do it. Here, Father, please fix it." Then wait quietly. He will work even if you feel nothing.

Don't try to cover a lot of attitudes in one prayer period. One at a time is enough. To reinforce your growth you may find several passages in Matthew relating to the same subject, or you may remain focused on one. *It is essential only to ask him to change you and to relax.* Don't berate yourself and don't take yourself by the throat determined to *do* something. Be a child. Let him. And when you make a ghastly discovery about yourself (he'll make sure you do when you're ready!), just remember that he's known it all along — and loves you most preciously.

Another possible practice/prayer for Kingdom attitudes is to try to feel your way into a new feeling. It's only a starter, and if you've never tried it you may find it awkward. But it can be fruitful. For example, what would it feel like to want the Kingdom in your every day so much that everything else came second (13:44-46)? For this moment of prayer, don't ask what it would cost or how it would affect your habits. Ask playfully how it would feel within you. Enjoy the feeling. Experience it as a pleasant attitude. Combine it with visualization if you wish, and put yourself in Jesus' presence to feel your desire for him. Let the feeling pervade you; ask him to deepen it.

The second kind of prayer with Matthew is behavioral prayer. It's a little tricky because you can behave "correctly" yet falsely. This was the Pharisees' problem, this doing without being. Today we know it can cause serious emotional difficulties. It certainly suppresses joy.

However, behavioral prayer is an experiment in walking along behind Jesus, enjoying our own "follow the leader." It is not to be an assignment worked over until we have it right and then presented to him. Practice like a toddler who is trying to walk with his or her parent. Be willing to be clumsy, so that he can show you the next step and hold your hand while you take it. For example, take 7:1-2. Christians have always honored mortification. This is one of the best mortifications around, but seldom practiced! Do it lightly with a gentle, keen perception of yourself. It need not be a miserable experience. It can be a discovery. If you practice gently for Jesus whom you love, you can laugh at yourself as you clamp a hand over your mouth. If you laugh at yourself while doing for him, you are at prayer.

Look through the Gospel again for more possibilities to embrace behavioral prayer. Some will suggest what not to do. Others, perhaps the harder ones, will be what *to* do, like 6:3-4 or 5:23-24. These too can be handled gently, an exploration for love of God. Before long the Kingdom's joy will begin to creep in at your inner edges. When it does, revel in it. It is truth. It is his.

Questions to Answer

Note: As you answer the questions given here, be specific. *Jot down the references from which your answers come.* Do not answer merely from "feelings" you already have about Jesus; make your answers come from the Gospel. Answering in this way will clarify both your own thought and your understanding of the Gospel itself.

If you are in a group, use the questions for discussion. Take time to look up the references each person has found. *Don't hesitate to write in your Bible.* No one will remember everything in the readings, so note your responses in the margins.

1. How does Matthew understand Jesus to be fulfillment of prophecy? (You may find it interesting to look up the quotations used by Matthew from the Old Testament. A handy tool for this purpose is *The New World Dictionary-Concordance to the New*

American Bible, a paperback book by World Publishing, 1970. To check Matthew's use of the Old Testament, you can also use the lettered footnotes on the pages of Matthew's Gospel in the *New American Bible* or the *Revised Standard Version.* For references of this kind, the *Jerusalem Bible* is also especially helpful.)

2. Did Jesus' teaching change the Old Law? If so, how?

3. Matthew calls Jesus the Messiah. What does that title mean in this Gospel?

4. What is the core of all Jesus' teaching? Find the references where he expresses it.

5. Do you think the teachings of Jesus are really practical? What are your reasons for your opinion?

6. What specific instructions does Jesus give about prayer? What other teachings can be related to prayer?

Suggestions for Family Use

Use any of the suggestions you find in this chapter.

If you are experimenting with memorization, Matthew is filled with short, important sayings. Matthew has even organized some of these sayings to make memorization easier. For example, see especially chapters 5, 6, and 7.

As a family, choose one or two principles from chapters 5, 6, 7, or 18 of Matthew that you plan to practice together for a week. Report back to each other. (The main meal of the day might be a good time to do this.) Ask each other: How is it going? What is hard? What is easy? How can I help you?

Be careful not to evaluate how well some other family member is doing. Remember Matthew 7:1.

You might want to let the above practice grow into a family prayer of petition. Bring to God whatever family problems are most apparent. Let each person contribute something to the petition. Pray your petition together.

Session Suggestions

If you are using this booklet for a 10-session series, here are suggestions for the two sessions on Matthew.

Session 1: Use the material in this chapter, *focusing on the passages in Matthew* that are referred to. Since so many passages are referred to, have the people present break up into small groups. Then divide the passages referred to into sections, one section for each small group.

Between sessions: Have each person privately read the entire Gospel of Matthew, with this booklet in hand as a guide.

Session 2: Focus on *prayer* with Matthew. Take Jesus' discourses and have everyone zero in on passages for *behavioral* prayer. (For examples of such passages, see page 36 in the section "Praying with Matthew.") After they have located these passages, give the group an opportunity to share their findings.

If you are using this booklet for a 20-session series, here are suggestions for the four sessions on Matthew.

Session 1: Read Matthew, using this booklet as a guide. In your Bible jot down the main points of each section outlined in this chapter. Discuss especially the Sermon on the Mount.

Session 2: Review the Gospel by a second reading. Answer and discuss Questions 1, 2, and 3 above.

Session 3: Read the discourses as suggested for prayer on page 35 in the section "Praying with Matthew." Experiment with daily prayer for Kingdom attitudes. Share experiences in the group.

Session 4: Find one or two practices for behavioral prayer. Experiment. Reread the discourses, then discuss Questions 4, 5, and 6.

3
The Gospel of Luke: The Mission of Jesus and His Holy Spirit

The Gospel of Luke bids us graciously to Jesus and yet shows respect for accuracy. His portrait of Jesus is pervaded with Jesus' own gentleness. In this Gospel, Jesus' tenderheartedness shines warmly on his contemporaries and on us too.

Author and Date

According to very early reports, Luke's Gospel (as well as its second half, Acts of the Apostles) was written by Luke who was a physician and a Gentile. We don't know how or when he became a Christian. He accompanied Paul on some of his journeys (see Acts 16:1-17; 20:5—21:18; 27:1—28:16). Paul appreciated Luke's presence while he was imprisoned in Rome (see Colossians 4:14 and Philemon, chapter 23). A tradition suggests that Luke also spent time in Ephesus where he might have known John and also Mary, Jesus' Mother. So Luke had much opportunity to hear the preaching and reminiscences of Jesus' earliest followers.

Luke probably wrote his Gospel and Acts about the same time Matthew was written, 80-85 A.D. The writer looks back to Jesus' time, having collected all available information and tradition. Then he creates an orderly and historical story for Theophilus, who may have been a Roman official (Luke 1:3-4).

Circumstances and Audience

Luke's larger world is like Matthew's, but Luke's readership is primarily Gentile like himself. He is less interested in Jesus' Jewish connections than in his worldwide significance. Notice, for example, the genealogy in 3:23-38. Luke traces Jesus' lineage back to Adam, the first human being, in contrast to Matthew who traces it to Abraham, the first Hebrew. Luke is generally inattentive to purely Jewish issues. Clearly, he writes for Gentiles — and literate ones, too, for scholars tell us his Greek is excellent.

Like Mark and Matthew, Luke presents Jesus to the faith-seeking reader. His devotion to Jesus is obvious. Luke emphasizes the mission of Jesus and its continuation in the Church through the Holy Spirit. The Holy Spirit is most prominent in Acts, but he holds a larger place in Luke than in any other Gospel. Especially in the first four chapters, the Holy Spirit is the motivating power behind events (1:16; 1:34-35; 1:42; 1:67; 2:26-27; 3:16; 3:22; 4:1; 4:14). Luke marks the start of Jesus' mission, points out its purposes, then follows its expansion from Palestine to the whole known world, climaxing in Rome. Luke's Jesus is impelled by his mission — a mission intended for the Gentiles from its beginnings, a mission of compassion especially to the poor, the lost, the outcasts. And Luke's Jesus has a unique sensitivity to the women around him. Let's accompany Luke as he explores Jesus' mission.

In the 50 years since Jesus' Resurrection there had been rivalry between Gentile and Jewish Christians. Indeed, the Jews did seem to have a better claim to Christ. But the movement of the Spirit (which Luke follows so happily in Acts) went out increasingly to Gentiles. Now in the 80s Gentile Christians may have urgently needed the assurance that they had had a place from the very beginning. Luke roots that certainty firmly in the inspired perception of Simeon (2:30-32) years before in Jesus' infancy. Luke does not believe that the Gentile Christian had a chance for Jesus only because the Jewish leadership rejected him. For Luke, Jesus' eternal purpose was to be Savior for all in the world. Jesus is a glory for the Jews, yes; but his light is for everyone everywhere. The participation of Gentiles in Christ is the fulfillment of God's original intention, not an accident of Jewish attitudes.

At Jesus' baptism (3:6) Luke reaffirms this conviction. He quotes Isaiah 40:3-5 to demonstrate God's long-term intention. Compare Matthew 3:3 which omits the verse about all mankind. Thus in Luke even John the Baptizer asserts that Jesus is for all people.

Mission to the Gentiles

Luke's Gospel shows a constant interest in Gentiles and their needs, although Jesus doesn't preach outside of Palestine. Gentiles are around him all the time, as indeed they must have been in that mixed Palestinian society. They hear him and they respond to him. In fact, sometimes the Gentiles seem to understand Jesus better than his own people do. Let's look at a few examples. You will want to examine the Gospel for other similar stories.

Early in Jesus' public ministry (4:16-27), in Nazareth, people ask skeptically whether this isn't their own carpenter's son. The strength of Jesus' self-defense indicates that it isn't the first time he has weighed his relationship to Gentiles. He knows already from Scripture that God sent his messengers to Gentiles and he too will go to them. So soon Jesus sets his purpose firmly against the prejudices and expectations of his own people, sensitively discerning the Father's loving purpose for Gentiles as well as Jews.

Jesus responds to all people (7:1-10). This Roman was known and loved by the Jews among whom he worked. He was a sensitive man himself, for he didn't impose his military presence on Jesus, as he had every legal right to do. He needed help. He recognized spiritual authority when he saw it and expected no superfluities: Jesus need only speak. For his part, Jesus goes readily, intending doubtless to enter the Roman home, even though it violated ritual purity laws and would render him unclean. But the Roman again anticipates him, insisting "Please don't." Jesus, openhearted to the man's character regardless of his nationality, reciprocates simply. He heals. And he likes the

Roman. The Roman trusts even more than the Israelites do. By the 80s such a memory would encourage and gladden Gentile Christians, helping them to be confident that it was their faith Jesus sought, not their origins.

Jesus steadfastly asserts that though the Kingdom was first offered to Jews it will be Gentiles who actually live in it. Take a look at 13:28-30. Jesus' immediate hearers are (understandably!) irritated. But for Luke's readers, Jesus' comment is great hope and support.

In 17:11-19 Luke tells us about Jesus healing ten lepers. The point often made for us is the ingratitude of the nine. But the point for Luke's readers and for Jesus was that only the despised Samaritan loved God enough to be grateful. One of the endlessly fascinating aspects of Scripture stories is that they enlighten us about several things. Here we find that ingratitude for love is not lovely. Furthermore, the one we hate may be the more loving one. Jesus flouts the bias of his time by healing all ten without asking who they are. Finally, Jesus' reaction to the Samaritan shows again his approval for personal quality above all else. Jesus still gives us much to live up to, doesn't he?

Even in Jesus' dying the Gentile is remembered, despite the fact that Gentiles have ordered his execution. The centurion in Luke who marvels at the manner in which Jesus dies exclaims over the innocence of Jesus' spirit (23:47). He had the integrity to speak out for justice, even though it was too late to do more.

Thus Luke describes Jesus' kindly relationship to Gentiles throughout his earthly life. Fifty years later, Gentile Christians are the backbone of the Church. Luke's writing must have reassured them deeply. To us, also, Luke brings this happy knowledge. We too are Gentiles. We have assumed that we have a place in Christ, and rightly. Still it is cheering to know that God intended it so from the beginning, that we are his adopted children because he wanted us and not merely by the default of someone else. Praise God for Luke's inspired insight!

Mission to the Poor and Outcasts

Jesus' interest in Gentiles heightens to compassion for the poor, the lost, the outcasts of his immediate society. Luke has a special affinity for Jesus' compassion. He sees in Jesus the great brooding, tender Spirit of the Father who seeks all misfits, all who don't quite belong, all who sin and experience guilt and confusion, and especially those who suffer poverty. Space limits our examples, but you can soon find others.

Luke grounds his theme again right in the beginning of Jesus' history. The barren wife (truly an outcast in Israelite society) bears a miraculous child, a prophet (1:7-25). Jesus' own Mother (1:50-53) rejoices that those with status in this world are set aside while those with nothing are exalted. An old widow in the Temple delights in Jesus' presentation there (2:36-38). Even when John the Baptizer preaches, it is not only "good" people who come to him but tax collectors and soldiers — outcasts all (3:12-14).

The tax collectors were generally despised for being collaborators with the Romans. They not only gathered the hated taxes but often overcharged their own people and pocketed the extra. Yet Luke's Jesus seeks out these very people to love and spends his time with them. He even asks one of them to be particularly close to him (5:27-32). You will want to read also 18:9-14 and likewise the familiar story of Zacchaeus in 19:1-10. Notice that Jesus nowhere implies that being a tax collector was a good thing. But with gentle perceptivity, he looks beyond the behavior, even beyond the morality of the situation, to find the child of God hidden there and win him to his Kingdom. He cared about him and others like him.

Our own society has no real equivalent to the tax collectors of first-century Palestine. But we do live among people whose moral behavior we may view with contempt. For example, people with shady sexual reputations are generally not sought out by upright churchgoers. Or those who have committed a crime, whether in or out of prison. Or the person whose value system cuts offensively across traditional standards. To all such people Jesus offered his daily attention, kindly and openly. No matter how out of place or how wrong they seemed, Jesus never hesitated to encircle them in his love. That meant even defending them sometimes. Luke 7:36-50 tells us about an immoral woman who came to touch Jesus, to express her love. He accepted her love and told the Pharisee that he, the Pharisee, was the confused one. In Jesus' presence, the woman was welcome to hold up her head and be herself. As for criminals, the only person to receive a promise of paradise from Jesus' own lips was a man who had been condemned to death (23:39-43).

Luke alone tells us the shining parables of the Father's compassion in chapter 15. The son who took his father's money and squandered it is often thought to be the main character. But for Jesus the main character is the father who is a figure of his own Father. The father gives his child freedom to waste what is his; the father waits longingly for his son's return home; the father doesn't reprimand the broken young man, but immediately — ahead of the boy himself — runs to hearten him. He honors him! The boy must have been a bit overwhelmed, but imagine the great freedom, the intense joy of the father! To Jesus, this is the One he called *Abba,* which doesn't mean "Father" but "Daddy." Luke's stories are poignant, aren't they? And still vibrant for us.

Who are usually considered the dregs of a society? Where standards are money-based, the poor come out as the lowest of all. But Jesus didn't see it that way. In fact, the poor were the focus of Jesus' special tenderness. In Luke 6:20-21 when Jesus begins his teaching on the Kingdom, he says the first people who know the joyousness of the Kingdom are the poor and the hungry. Luke does not give this a spiritual meaning (as Matthew does). Jesus suggests that precisely those who are not joyous in the material world have the most potential for spiritual joy. Do you accept that? Do you think that "we must feed their bodies before we can feed their souls"?

Jesus' appreciation for generosity in the poor has an exceptional warmth about it. He knows how it is with them. He makes an eloquent comment in 21:1-4. Once again Jesus looks so caringly into a person's inner life, into the heart, the motivation. This woman's poverty only enhances her gift. The quantity means nothing. You may want to pause a moment here. Visualize what Jesus is doing, how he looks, the expression on his face. Has this woman brought him a flash of delight?

In Luke 14:16-24 and 16:19-31, Jesus tells two parables about the Kingdom and the poor. He says that the rich are too distracted to enter the Kingdom. So the poor and the sick — regarded by their contemporaries as being under divine judgment for sin — would be the Kingdom's participants. The poor man who lay right at the gate of the rich man's house was a familiar scene to Jesus' listeners. In the 20th century, the poor rarely lie at our front door, but none of us has to drive very far to find people living in poverty. Will they enter the Kingdom before us? Is it possible that possessions may rob us of Kingdom joy? The least we can do is to emulate Jesus' own caring for those who do not have enough. As you read Luke's Gospel, you may feel that Jesus is not as much concerned to feed the poor as he is to love them. Mother Teresa of Calcutta has said so often that the real starvation of humanity is not for food, but for love. She got the idea from Jesus.

Mission to Women

Jesus' relationships to women have long been recognized in Luke. Luke mentions women and their contributions to Jesus much more often than the other Gospels do. Jesus is sensitive to them as human beings. He makes them friends. Look at 7:11-15. Jesus works a miracle for this distressed woman, but it is not basically a power display. He hurts for her. He knows the dreadful situation of widows in his world — she may starve to death if her only son is gone. So he goes to her first, "Don't cry. It'll be all right." Jesus is, in modern language, a real "softie." We can be glad. Just so gentle is he with us.

In 8:1-3 Luke informs us that a group of women traveled with Jesus and the Twelve and cared for them. Again at his death, women are present (23:49) and they look after his body (23:55-56). Because of their concern to do that, they are the first to learn of his Resurrection (24:1-11). So among Jesus' constant companions are women whom he loves and whose care he accepts graciously and thankfully.

Two of Jesus' closest friends are women: Mary and Martha who live in Bethany close to Jerusalem. When he comes to the city, he stays in their home (10:38-42).

Luke's mere inclusion of Jesus' words to women indicates that Jesus loved them: 13:1-13; 21:23; 23:27-30. In Jesus' society women didn't have a full place. Devout Jewish men said a morning prayer thanking God for not having made them women. Jesus spoke freely to women, even in the streets, and healed those who needed him. In Luke's educated Gentile world, women had a fuller place; and he saw and appreciated Jesus' attitude. Luke's Gentile perspective on Jesus enriches us too.

It is significant that Luke gathers these three groups — Gentiles, outcasts, and women — at the foot of the Cross. You may want to reread Luke's account of the crucifixion (23:26-24:54) and recall them. Just as Jesus had loved them and attended to them during his public life, so they receive his redemption, the completion of his mission, though they didn't know then just how tremendous it was.

The fulfillment of Jesus' mission took place after the Resurrection, through the action of the Holy Spirit. Luke tells that story in Acts, where again Gentiles and outcasts and women find their place. Read Acts to get the story firsthand.

Praying with Luke

Luke mentions prayer oftener than any other Gospel writer. Most frequently Jesus is praying. This dimension of Jesus' life reaffirms that he was as a human being closely united with the Father. He spent time alone with the Father whenever he could

(5:16). Luke portrays Jesus exulting joyfully in the Spirit, speaking to the Father (10:21). Watching Jesus, we implore him along with his disciples, "Please teach us to pray."

Jesus sought the Father for total sustenance of his whole being. In prayer he was nourished. Prayer likewise offers us the complete nurture of the Father. Recognizing the power and love available to Jesus in the Father, we surmise that the basic stance of Jesus' prayer was receptivity. He was open to the Father.

We may assume we are also receptive. After all, don't we constantly ask for things? Yet we are often so busy begging that we forget to sit back and receive what he gives.

Luke, who knows Jesus as a great giver, will help you grow in receptivity. Choose one of his stories of Jesus' responsiveness to people, perhaps the one you most enjoy. Quietly put yourself in place of the person to whom Jesus shows his love. Let him give you that same attention. Feel his gentleness with you. Be deeply still and let him love you. Just let him. Be open to him, resting — and *like* being loved. Allow the pleasure of it to seep into your hidden inner corners. Do nothing but receive him. Take a different story for each period of prayer. Soon you will be aware of a fragile but inexpressibly comforting sense of being sustained, being held up, being carried deep within yourself. Rejoice, for this is one entrance to the Kingdom.

Jesus also sought definite guidance from the Father in his big decisions and complete acceptance of the Father's will in all he did. We see it most vividly just before the Passion (22:39-44). *You too want guidance from the Father,* as well as the strength to accept his lovely gifts — which are, unexpectedly, sometimes more difficult to accept than the not-so-lovely ones. Here the examples of Jesus at prayer before major decisions can tell us something (6:12; 9:18-22; 9:28-36; and others). Think of the decisions that you now face, big or little. Do you want his guidance? Once you ask for it, do you relax to listen to him? Surely half of the time we spend seeking guidance should be spent listening. The Father really doesn't need long details. He knows them already. But we do need to hear him. So make a list of your pending decisions. Then ponder over Luke 5:1-11 as you take your list to him. Expect answers. Listen for them.

Today people are rediscovering the prayer of praise. *If our first approach to God with Luke is receptivity, certainly that calls for completion in praise.* Joyful response to the Father is especially encouraged by Luke. Look again at 10:21-22 where Jesus himself is exulting. Enjoy the spontaneity with which Jesus turns to praise the Father. Consider similar spontaneous delight in God in your own life. Help it grow by practicing praise of him. Use Luke 1:46-55 or 1:68-79 as starters. You may want to search the Gospel for all its joyful words, such as *rejoice, blessed, exalt, exult, happy.* Focus on these passages in your prayer period. Or use them to open and close your prayer time.

As you receive God's love in your daily prayer, as you follow his guidance in your decisions, and as you give him thanks for himself, you will increasingly know that God is very active in your life. Your circumstances will begin to reflect his action, your inner life will speak of his presence there, your relationships with others will become more satisfying.

Then you will want to share the goodness of God. Jesus taught his followers to be witnesses for him. The beginning of chapter 10 tells of his sending them out. In his final words to them, he again calls them his witnesses (24:28). Remember that witnessing was not an abstraction for those early Christians. They were thrilled by what they had seen, what they knew from their own experience. It is pointless to try to witness for God until you have known him, until you find him wonderful. Telling people what they should believe is powerless. The witness that brings Jesus to others is the word of experience, the reflection of all his significance for you. It is important that you share him, first of all for your hearer, but also for yourself. You continue to receive of God only as you continuously give. So pass along his goodness to you. This too is prayer.

Questions to Answer

Note: As you answer the questions given here, be specific. Jot down the references from which your answers come. If you are in a group, use the questions for discussion. Don't hesitate to write in your Bible.

1. Luke is well known for the parables. You may want to study them separately. Look for one main message in each parable.

2. Who in our society correspond to the poor and the outcasts of Jesus' society? What would Jesus offer them? Give references from Luke.

3. How are we to understand the proximity of joy and suffering in the Gospels? Find examples in Luke.

4. To what extent was Jesus aware of his own mission and its characteristics?

5. Does Luke's collection of Jesus' teachings seem as challenging as Matthew's? Or more so? Compare Luke 6:17-49 with chapters 5 through 7 of Matthew.

Suggestions for Family Use

Together, stop and think deeply about Jesus' love for each individual in your family. What qualities does Jesus love in each person? Have each person take pen and paper and make a list of each family member's beautiful qualities. After listing one another's qualities, express your love for each person in words, and also nonverbally; give each other an embrace or a kiss. Make a point of being really glad to *receive* the love each person expresses for you. Don't hurry when you do this. Take all the time in the world.

Look up and discuss the meaning of the word *gentile.* Discuss the following questions:

● Who are "gentiles" today? Who are the misfits among the people you come in contact with?

● Does Jesus have a mission to these people? What is that mission?

• How can your family help Jesus with his mission to these people? (In answering this question, look closely at the people you meet at school, in the neighborhood, at church.)

• How would Jesus treat those who just don't belong? How can your family be like him, how can you *be* him to these people?

Using pen and paper again, have each person make a list of the reasons your family has for loving Jesus. Then have each person share at least one reason with the group. Praise Jesus together, perhaps standing in a circle and holding hands.

Use any other suggestions you find in this chapter.

Session Suggestions

If you are using this booklet for a 10-session series, here are suggestions for the two sessions on Luke.

Session 1: The first session could cover this booklet chapter, focusing especially on Jesus' mission to the Gentiles, outcasts, and women. Use Question 2 for discussion.

Session 2: This session could be based on a reading of the whole Gospel of Luke. Discuss the prayer of praise and the prayer of witnessing. How do praise and witnessing nourish each other?

If you are using this booklet for a 20-session series, here are suggestions for the four sessions on Luke.

Session 1: Read Luke's Gospel and the first section of this chapter (up to the heading "Mission to the Poor and Outcasts"). Discuss the universality of Jesus' mission to the Gentiles.

Session 2: Using the second part of this chapter, collect the references in Luke for Jesus' mission to outcasts and to women. Discuss Questions 2 and 3 above.

Session 3: Begin to pray with Luke. Share your experiences. Discuss: How do you create receptivity? How do you handle distractions? Is it dishonest to praise him when you are hurting?

Session 4: Review the whole Gospel of Luke. Discuss Questions 1, 4, and 5 above.

4
The Gospel of John: Union with Jesus and the Father

An adult Scripture student of mine said recently, "Studying John was like drinking champagne all the time." Her enthusiasm has been shared by countless Christians ever since the Gospel of John was written. John is the brilliant work of an excellent mind and, more importantly, the result of a vibrant spiritual life grounded in a personal relationship with Jesus Christ. Perhaps in no other book of the Bible can we see more clearly that Scripture demands our very best thought as well as our deepest prayer.

John is different from the other three Gospels (the Synoptics). Its order of events is different, it puts several long discourses on Jesus' lips, its pattern of composition is unique, and the proportion (about half the Gospel) given to the Passion is longer. Because of these differences, scholars believe John presents another body of tradition than that of the Synoptics. It supplies a special picture of Jesus as well as of the Christian community. How impoverished we would be without John!

Date, Author, Audience

The general agreement among scholars is that this Gospel was written in the 90s A.D. It is the latest Gospel, coming 60 years after the Resurrection. The Christian Church has by this time developed some organization, some sense of direction and identity. Problems it also has, one of which is the vociferous opposition of the synagogue, especially since the Jews expelled Jewish Christians altogether.

Scholars no longer think that John, the son of Zebedee (one of the Twelve), actually wrote the Gospel himself. But many do believe he was the guiding spirit in the community where this body of tradition was preserved. The general view of the formation of the Gospel is something like this: The Beloved Disciple may have been John, son of Zebedee. He gathered a community of Christians and shared his memory and insight of Jesus. Together they collected and kept the tradition about Jesus. The Beloved Disciple is the major influence on the Evangelist who actually wrote the Gospel, whose name we don't know. After he wrote, a redactor (an editor) judiciously added to and rearranged the material a little. One example of his work is chapter 21. Look at 20:30-31. Doesn't it sound like a conclusion? Chapter 21 was added by the redactor.

In this booklet, "John" refers to the Evangelist (the writer) who was not one of the Twelve. But remember that John reflects the spiritual penetration and memory of the Beloved Disciple. (This is somewhat similar to Mark's relation to Peter's preaching.)

John's audience is primarily Gentile, largely already Christian, but he looks also to a missionary objective. In 20:31 John defines the purpose of his writing: that people may believe in Jesus as Son of God and receive his fullness of life. Let that be your purpose, too, in your reading and prayer with John: to trust him more and participate in his life.

The Book of Signs

John is divided into sections. The first section (chapters 1 through 12) is called today the "Book of Signs" because here John gives us signs that Jesus performed to reveal himself. (Chapter 8:1-11 is a genuine memory of Jesus, but out of place in John.) Each sign is followed by a discourse which enlarges on the significance of the sign. The second section (chapters 13 through 20) is called the "Book of Glory." It is the story and meaning of the Passion, Death, and Resurrection of Jesus.

John writes symbolically. He preserves historical tradition, but uses it to disclose a deep meaning. The beauty, the challenge, the invitation in John unfold as we look below the obvious to find these underlying meanings.

Right away John announces (1:1-18) the subject of his Gospel: the Word, the Son, the only one who has revealed the Father. Verses 10-12 summarize Jesus' ministry: He came to his own people, and was unrecognized and rejected; but those who did accept him he empowered to become children of God.

The Book of Signs then opens by placing Jesus in perspective. First it clarifies the position of John the Baptizer (1:19-27). Then, in 1:34 (and through the words of his disciples in the following verses), it tells who Jesus is. Watch the progression of their understanding: rabbi (1:38), then Messiah (1:41), then the fulfillment of Old Testament expectations (1:45), and finally Son of God and King of Israel (1:49). The key line is Jesus' response to the disciples in 1:39, "Come and see." That is the invitation of the whole Gospel: Come to Jesus, see who he is — and then remain with him, as those two followers did (1:39).

The First Sign

In order to enable his followers to "see," Jesus performs signs that show his glory. John gives us seven of them. The first one is the changing of water into wine at Cana (2:1-12). In this story we learn several things about Jesus. First, his primary concern is the will of the Father and the Father's timing (the hour, 2:4). Then the water jars (2:6) open a favorite theme of John's. He sees Jesus as completely replacing all the Jewish laws and feasts and observances. The custom in this case is ritual purification; but Jesus uses those jars for something better, for new wine symbolizing the Kingdom. Further, the whole wedding setting is reminiscent of the feast at the end of time, when the Anointed One will come and everyone will sit down at his table. To climax it all, the headwaiter says (2:10) this choicest wine was "kept until now." To John this means that Jesus is the One only now sent from God to initiate the Kingdom.

Notice how little interest John shows in the mechanics of the miracle. In verse 9 he says only a phrase, "water made wine." Not interested in sensationalism, he penetrates to the interior symbolic meaning of Jesus' acts.

Between the first and second signs, John describes several people who come to Jesus. Reading these stories is like ascending a ladder of faith, topped off by the second sign. The first rung occurs in 2:13-22. Here the Jewish leadership does not believe in Jesus, nor do his followers really believe his *word* at this time (2:20, 22). But some people do believe in him, *because of the signs* only (2:23). The second rung is Nicodemus (3:1-21) who comes to Jesus because of the signs (3:2), but persists in his misunderstanding of Jesus' words. The third rung is John the Baptizer (3:22-30) who believes joyfully in Jesus' messiahship (3:28-29). At the fourth rung of faith the Samaritan woman (4:4-42) believes in Jesus' *words* to her as she hears truth that she recognizes (4:17-19,29), then delights in him as prophet and Messiah.

The Second, Third, and Fourth Signs

The top rung of the ladder is the second sign Jesus performs. He cures the official's son. The key sentence is 4:50b, "He put his trust in the *word* Jesus spoke." For John, Jesus himself is that Word. This is quite in contrast to believing in Jesus because of signs (4:48). Note too that the boy is near death and Jesus gives him life. John invites you again: Come, see, believe, and receive life.

In Jesus' third sign, he restores to life the paralytic at Bethesda after 38 years beside the pool (5:1-30). Jesus, being one with the Father, is capable of giving life — indeed, he is expected to do so (5:19-21). For John, though, life is more than simple physical existence. It is eternal life in Jesus, union with him and the Father, participation in the very life of God (5:25-26). In verse 25, "dead" means *spiritually* dead. Jesus did this sign on the Sabbath, thereby demonstrating that he superceded the Sabbath (5:17).

The fourth sign is the multiplication of the loaves in 6:1-15. The passage is so full of allusions, each rich with background, that we never tire of it. The sign's inner significance is explained in the discourse, 6:32-58. You are already familiar with its implications for the Eucharist. An interesting note: scholars say that the word used for "pieces" in 6:13 is the same Greek word used in early Christian liturgy for "hosts." Other connections are interesting, too. The event happens about Passover time. Passover celebrated the Exodus, the beginning of the Hebrews as a people, and it was one of their greatest feasts. In the discourse, the references to Moses and manna intensify this parallel. In verses 41 and 43, the term *murmuring* (or, in some translations, *grumbling* or *complaining*) is a rarely used word, but see Exodus 15:24 and 16:2. By such connections, Jesus daringly affirms that he replaces the Passover. He even surpasses the work of Moses, since the Father gives the real heavenly bread and Jesus himself *is* that bread.

As with the other signs, this one inspires amazed belief in 6:14. The prophet is part of the end-time expectations, and the people are eager to make him their king (6:15).

Once again, John is uninterested in the mechanics of the miracles; the disciples simply collect the leftovers.

The Fifth, Sixth, and Seventh Signs

The fifth sign, 6:16-21, gives the setting for the discourse and also introduces a new theme, the "I am" theme. (For references to this theme in John's Gospel, look ahead to page 57 in this booklet.)

The explanatory discourse (6:26-66) affects the faith of Jesus' followers. Some find it impossible to make sense of him anymore, and they depart. Only the closest ones remain, and Peter's statement (6:68-69) means that they no longer depend on signs for belief. They trust his word and believe in him. How much they have grown since the Cana wedding (2:11)!

Chapters 7 and 8 prepare us for the sixth sign. Jesus is in Jerusalem again, this time for the Feast of Tabernacles. The Feast was originally a harvest festival which developed historical meanings about the kingship of Yahweh. At night the Temple courtyards are illuminated with great torches. On the last day a great libation of water was poured and Jesus stood amid the celebration and cried out, "If anyone thirsts, let him come to me . . . 'From within him rivers of living water shall flow'" (7:37-38). Then in 8:12 (was it at dusk just as the torches were lighted?) Jesus declares that he himself is light that conquers all darkness. Thus is the festival superceded again by Jesus, and its meaning (kingship) appropriated by him.

Jesus performs the sixth sign (9:1-41) to demonstrate his claim to be light: he gives sight to a man born blind. He "enlightens" the man's living. It's intriguing that Baptism in the early Church was sometimes called enlightenment. Chapter 9 is dramatic and even humorous. Enjoy it. Jesus' hearers were increasingly taking sides (9:13-16). The situation of the 90s is reflected in 9:22-23. It wouldn't have happened in Jesus' own time, because then nobody had a reason to fear expulsion. In the 90s it was a fact. Then 9:35-39 would also be doubly significant, implying that those who are thrown out of the synagogue come to Jesus for true light.

The seventh and last of Jesus' signs is the raising of Lazarus in chapter 11. It is magnificent drama. Jesus proves that he is life (even while he himself is on the way to death). But only trust in Jesus results in his life within. Look at 11:23-27. Martha trusts, though she has no idea what Jesus is going to do.

The results of this final sign are even greater division among people and the decision of the Sanhedrin to get rid of Jesus (11:45-57). Here we see one of John's neatest techniques. He puts the truth in the mouth of Jesus' opponents, making the whole scene ironic: verse 48 — both of these things actually happened; verses 50 and 52 — this is the real meaning of Jesus' death, though Caiaphas certainly didn't mean it that way.

These then are Jesus' signs in John. Each one is full of meanings. Hardly a sentence is there for its own sake. We've touched them only lightly. You will surely want to go back to them and search them more thoroughly. A fuller commentary on John's Gospel — there are many available — will be of help to you. So will prayer with John.

Themes and Key Words

You may also approach John thematically. By studying the signs you have followed this theme: Come, see, trust, and receive life. Other themes are a bit simpler to detect. You just look for a key word or phrase. One of these is *"I am."* Most of the time in John, Jesus uses "I am" as a title. That title is the meaning of the Hebrew word for God (see Exodus 3:14). Put on Jesus' tongue it is tantamount to affirming his divinity — which is precisely why the Jews are out to get him. (It also explains 18:6.) Here are the references for this term: 8:24,28,58;13:19— in these it can refer only to the divine name; 6:20 and 18:5 are used as in the Old Testament; 6:35,51; 8:12; 9:5; 10:7,9; 10:11,14; 14:6; 15:1,5 are semidivine uses and imply the divine participation in the Son.

Other key words are *light* (or light-darkness); *life;* Jesus' *hour* indicates the time determined by the Father for his glorification; *word* or words, often with the double meaning of language-words and the divine Word. To trace these themes, color-code them and mark the key words with highliners as you read through the Gospel. To explore the themes:

1. Follow the sequence of one theme from early in the Gospel to the end. Do you see new meaning as you go?

2. Notice the context of each reference (sign or discourse? explanation or event?) and its overall meaning.

3. Does Jesus explain the theme? How does the key word relate to what precedes or follows?

4. Do the themes relate to each other? Are they used in the same passage? Does one help explain another? How?

Be sure to jot down your discoveries in your Bible margin. John's complexity will make you glad you did!

The Book of Glory: Passion and Resurrection

All the themes and all the signs culminate in the great reality of the Passion/Death/Resurrection (chapters 13 through 20). It completes Jesus' whole ministry and actually provides all he has promised to his disciples. In one grand, glory-filled hour, Jesus *does* unmistakably all that he has been showing in the signs, promising in the discourses, and teaching to his disciples. Until now, Jesus has spoken and acted for all. Now everything is for "his own," the believers.

His final glorious hour begins in a position that could hardly be described as glorious (13:1-17): On the floor in front of his disciples, he washes their dirty feet. This action in John takes the place of the institution of the Eucharist in the Synoptics. John takes the Eucharist for granted, and offers a fuller explanation of its meaning by using another memory about Jesus. Eucharist presupposes a loving readiness to do all things, anything, to encourage fullness of life in another person. It means serving just as a slave serves.

Further, discipleship is a receiving from Jesus. We cannot communicate life to others until we have it ourselves; since it is not our own, we must receive it from him. And the way he gives it to us is by dying. So we know what Peter's problem is (13:6-9). Self-sufficiency will never bring us fullness of life. Fullness of life comes only in union with Jesus. Union with Jesus is only receivable; it is not earnable or achievable. We as followers can never say of life "I've gained it," but only "Yes, thank you, Lord!"

The major themes of this discourse (chapters 14 through 17) interpret Jesus' trial, harassment, death, Resurrection. For John, these are one event, have one meaning, are one act of Jesus. It is all glorification.

Notice that in the whole event (chapters 18 through 20) Jesus is not a victim. All our songs about Jesus the Victim may contain truth, but John wouldn't like them! For him, Jesus is in absolute control. Look at these points:

In 18:4 Jesus delivers himself.

In 18:11 he announces his determination to continue.

In 18:20-21,23 his words are hardly obsequious; his whole discussion with Pilate in 18:34-37 is a proclamation of his own kingship.

What calm certainty in the Father Jesus shows by being undefensive with Pilate in 19:9,11.

Unlike the picture presented by the Synoptics, Jesus carries his Cross alone in 19:17.

Hanging on the Cross, Jesus takes care of his Mother and his followers in 19:26-27.

He says he is thirsty only to fulfill the Scripture in 19:28; and finally, there is no cry of abandonment — Jesus declares his work finished and he delivers his own spirit to God in 19:30. Jesus is every moment the master who gives, who controls his own choices, never a victim of any circumstances (see also 10:17-18).

Glory, in Scripture, means the manifestation of God's presence among his people. It is divine self-revelation. This is precisely what happens in Jesus' glorification: he reveals himself. The essence of this revelation is written on the Cross (19:19). In 19:34, Jesus' revelation becomes life for everyone. Now all Jesus promised is fulfilled.

Then John tells us that warm story of Mary Magdalene and the resurrected Jesus (20:11-18). The dialogue reveals Jesus: "Who are you looking for?" balances Jesus' first invitation in 1:39. Mary wants to be with Jesus so intensely that when he merely speaks her name her arms are around him instantly. Jesus gently disentangles her and says, "Go . . . and tell." Her announcement is "I have seen Jesus!" Jesus had invited all to see him, had revealed himself fully in his glorification, and now his follower has seen. In the story of Thomas (20:24-29) his follower believes because he has seen. Then Jesus takes Christians one more step. He assures his joy and life to those who believe without seeing. Sight is, after all, only a step to the trust in him that opens us to his life.

Praying with John

More than any other Gospel, John brings us to prayer. To become one with Jesus is the disciple's whole hope, whole desire. That can happen only as you receive him in prayer, as you let him communicate his life to you. The Prologue (1:1-18) and Jesus' discourses are excellent springboards for prayer. Through them you are invited to touch him heart to heart.

The discourses often seem to move in circles. They give the impression of someone trying to describe a collage. This is a Semitic thought pattern, but for us it suggests meditation and reflection, rather than exposition of ideas. John's composition springs from years of meditative experience with Jesus. That's why the discourses are so conducive to depth in your own prayer.

The content of each discourse could, obviously, be partly described. Allusions can be explained and thought patterns pointed out. But in them is a profundity of mystery that does not wholly yield to examination. That mystery is the love of the Father as you receive it from Jesus in deep prayer. Nothing written here or anywhere can do that for you. You must pray.

To help you, here are a few phrases from each discourse as starters for your prayer. Then a method is suggested.

• 1:1-18, especially verses 3-5 (everything good is promised to you in Jesus Christ) and verses 11-12,14 (the Father is all hope and all love and he is yours).

• 3:5-21,31-36, especially verses 5-6 (natural birth does not in itself bring you to the Kingdom), verses 16-18 (belief in Jesus frees you from judgment), and verse 8 (complete freedom of the Spirit).

• 4:10-38, especially verses 23-24 (through Jesus' gift of life, true worship of the Father becomes possible) and verse 34 (doing the Father's will is fully nourishing).

• 5:19-47, especially verse 24 (the believer already has eternal life) and, throughout, you see the loving union of Jesus with the Father.

• 6:26-58, especially verse 27 (the goal of the believer's life and efforts), and verse 29 (the real work of every Christian) and verse 51 (anyone who takes Jesus unto himself has fullness of life).

• 8:12-58, especially verses 28-29 (Jesus is divine and his obedience to the Father is perfect), verse 47 (participation in God means communication with God), and verse 54 (God is the source of Jesus' self-revelation).

• 10:1-38, especially verse 9 (Jesus is the security for the believer), verses 10b-11 (Jesus gives himself totally to whoever trusts him).

• 12:44-50, especially verses 44-46 (Jesus is the way to the Father because they live in perfect union).

• Chapters 14 through 17, especially 14:1 (you can relax if you believe in Jesus), 14:12-13 (your potential as a believer is unlimited), 14:23 (you are never alone), 14:27 (here is the peace of mind usually sought everywhere else), 15:5-7 (Jesus wants you to bear fruit, but he will do it through you), 15:9-11 (he has such love for you, and it's for joy), 15:18-20 (count on being separated from your world if you belong to Jesus), 16:13-14 (the Spirit will be the communicator of Jesus to you; plan on it), 16:20-22 (Jesus' whole work is for your joy, so don't be deceived), 16:27 (rest in this one!), 17:9-10 (Jesus' unity with the Father is accomplished in you), 17:20-23 (your purpose for living and the purpose of the Church), 17:26 (the goal of Jesus' Death/Resurrection is in you).

The prayer pattern here suggested is simple to learn, contemplative, although not always easy to do. You can, of course, use it with any Scripture, but it seems made for the Gospel of John. Do it lightly, adventurously, ready to explore in the Spirit.

First, find a quiet place where you will not be interrupted. Eliminating all distractions, find a room where you will be assured of solitude. Then choose and locate your Scripture passage, keeping it handy. You may follow the discourse references above.

Then settle into a comfortable position. You may lie flat on your back or prone, or you may prefer a good chair. Only one caution: Be sure your back is straight or you will soon begin to squirm. Take a few minutes to relax as completely as you can. An easy way to relax is to take a few deep breaths, then talk to your muscles. Begin with your toes and deliberately relax each set of muscles all the way to the top of your head. Then quickly recheck your shoulders, your face, and your tongue. Let your attitude be relaxed too. Be pleasant with yourself.

Now turn your attention to God. Become aware of his Presence with you and within you. Thank him, first of all, for who he is, for who you are, and for this time together. Be still. Let your awareness of him intensify.

Turn to your Scripture passage. *Read very slowly, alertly.* When a word or phrase seems to speak to you, stop. Let that phrase rest in your mind. You may repeat it slowly, gently, over and over. Be free from applications, lessons, and resolutions. Here, now, just let the Word of God *be* within you. Be at ease. Don't worry if you feel nothing. He is here. Be quiet enough not to block his way. *Remain with one Scripture phrase as long as it retains its vitality for you.* Then, and only then, move gently to the next one. If you spend all of your prayer time with one phrase, that's good. You are after depth, not coverage!

When your time is over, *close your prayer with hearty thanksgiving,* especially for whatever happened in your prayer period. You may not even know what it was; but remember, you are the receiver. The doer is the Good Shepherd. He is taking care of your inner pasture, so you can well thank him in confidence.

Questions to Answer

Note: As you answer the questions given here, be specific. Jot down the references from which your answers come. If you are in a group, use the questions for discussion. Don't hesitate to write in your Bible.

1. What is the place of love in John's Gospel? List references to support your answer.

2. According to John, how can we experience union with the Father?

3. Who is Jesus?

4. What is your favorite passage in John? Why?

5. Compare and contrast the Passion in John (chapters 18 and 19) with the Passion in Luke (chapters 22 and 23). Which differences do you think are most significant? Why?

Suggestions for Family Use

Follow this booklet chapter together. When you get to chapter 13 of John's Gospel, plan a family foot washing. Read the story together; discuss its meaning. Then do the foot washing. To be sure each individual both washes someone's feet and is washed, sit in a circle. Pass a basin (or bucket) and towel all the way around. Finish with a prayer and sharing of feelings.

Read and discuss chapter 15 of John's Gospel. On a large sheet of paper, draw a large vine. Put Jesus' name on the main stem. Then have each family member write his or her name on one of the branches. Pictures could go there, too. On the remaining branches write the names of friends, relatives, etc.

Children are capable of learning the pattern of quiet prayer outlined in "Praying with John." If you want to pray in this way as a family, you can do it as follows. Relax together, all at the same time. Then close your eyes and pray silently for 5 to 10 minutes. Afterwards, share the experience. Discuss:

• How did you feel?

• What did you discover?

• Did you have any distractions? If so, what did you do about them?

Don't attempt to evaluate the experience until you have done it a few times. Just share and appreciate. Then give him thanks together.

Session Suggestions

Session 1: This session could revolve around the Book of Signs (chapters 1 through 12), with this booklet chapter (up to the heading "The Book of Glory: Passion and Resurrection") as guide. Be alert to Question 3 and discuss it if you have time.

Session 2: This session could concentrate on the Book of Glory (chapters 13 through 20). Discuss Question 5.

If you are using this booklet for a 20-session series, here are suggestions for the four sessions on John's Gospel.

Session 1: Read the entire Gospel, looking for the themes suggested in this booklet chapter under the heading "Themes and Key Words." Discuss the meaning of the themes along with Questions 1 and 3 above.

Session 2: Read the Book of Signs (chapters 1 through 12 of John's Gospel), with this booklet chapter (up to the heading "The Book of Glory: Passion and Resurrection") as guide. Discuss Question 3.

Session 3: Read the Book of Glory (chapters 13 through 20 in John's Gospel), using this booklet chapter as guide. Discuss Question 5.

Session 4: Read the entire Gospel of John, with a view to answering Question 1. Discuss Question 1, and save time for sharing on Question 4.

To climax all your reading and prayer with John, and to close this adventure in the Scripture, meditate on John 21:1-14. Jesus has returned to the place where he first met these disciples, the shore of Galilee. They are fishing. After letting them know by his sheer abundant giving that he's there, he calls them in for breakfast on the beach. Why not join them? There's no better company anywhere, and hardly anything tastes better than fresh-caught fried fish. You may discover, as you eat Jesus' cooking, that he is already yours in a new and magnificent way — and that indeed you will never be alone, for his love and joy are your eternal possession. Praise him!